State Shapes
State Shapes
State Shapes
State Shapes
Shapes

State Shapes
State Shapes
State Shapes
State Shapes
State Shapes
State Shapes
State Shapes
State Shapes
State Shapes
State Shapes
State Shapes
State Shapes
State Shapes
State Shapes
State Shapes
State Shapes
State Shapes

Published by
Black Dog & Leventhal Publishers, Inc.
151 West 19th Street
New York, NY 10011

Distributed by
Workman Publishing Company
225 Varick Street
New York, NY 10014

Designed by 27.12 design, ltd.

Manufactured in China

l k j i h g

www.blackdogandleventhal.com

Library-of-Congress Cataloging-in-Publication Data

Bruun, Erik A., 1961-
California / by Erik Bruun.
p. cm. -- (State Shapes)

Summary: Presents the history, important people, and famous places of the
Golden State, as well as miscellaneous facts about California today.

ISBN-13: 978-1-57912-100-6
1. California--Juvenile literature. [1. California.] I. Title.

F861.3 .B78 2000

979.4--dc21   00-024687

CALIFORNIA

BY ERIK BRUUN

illustrated by

RICK PETERSON

BLACK DOG
& LEVENTHAL
PUBLISHERS
NEW YORK

PACIFIC
OCEAN

REDWOOD
EMPIRE

1

S

SAN
FRANCIS

SANTA
CRU

CALIFORNIA

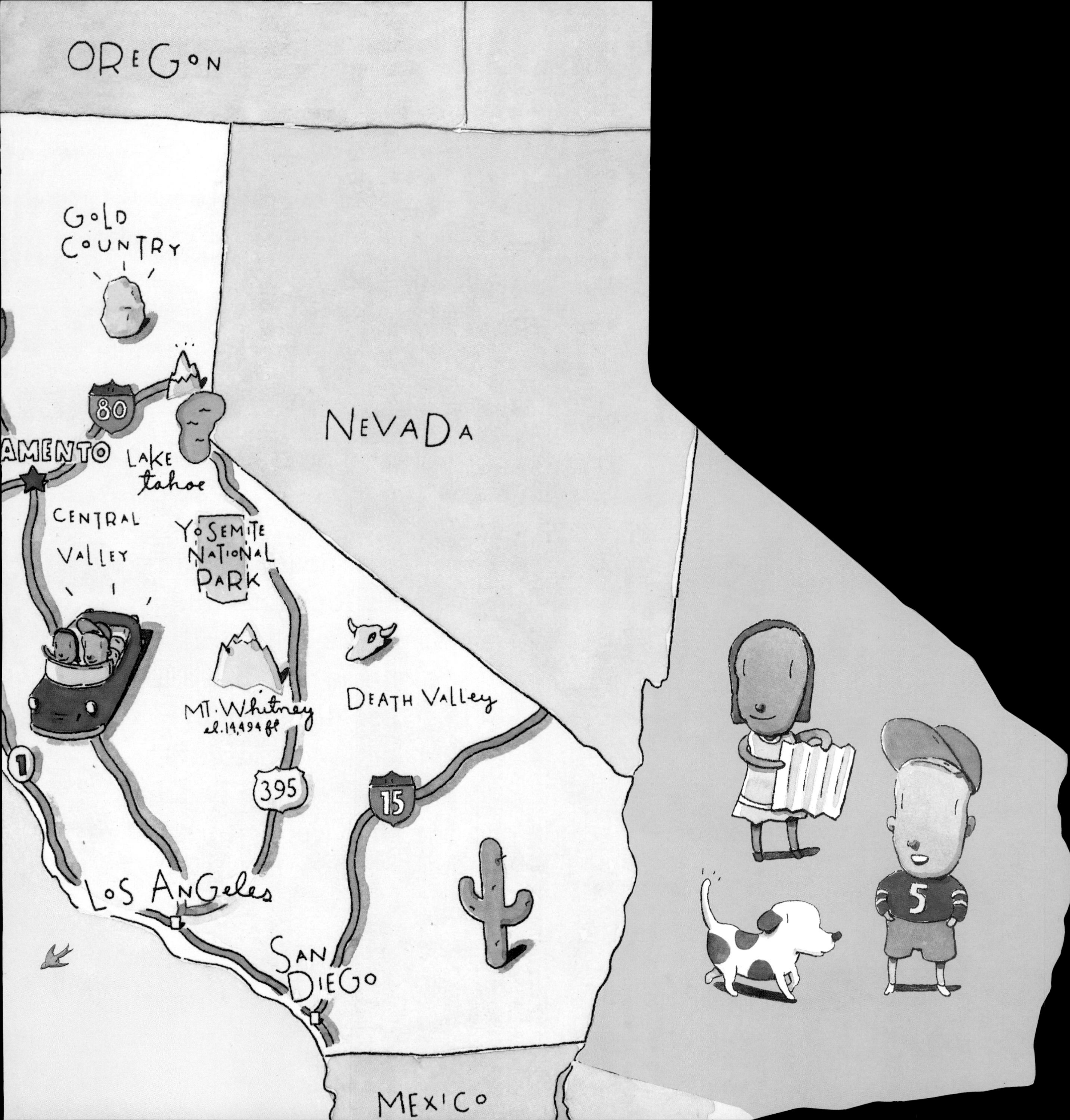
OREGON
GOLD COUNTRY
80
AMENTO
LAKE tahoe
NEVADA
CENTRAL VALLEY
YOSEMITE NATIONAL PARK
MT. Whitney el. 14,494 ft
DEATH Valley
1
395
15
LOS AnGeles
SAN DIEGO
5
MEXICO

Hi. I'm Carla Sanchez, your guide to the great state of California! California has more people than any other state and is the third largest in the Union. Its factories produce more computers, medical instruments and airplanes than any other state.

California has the world's tallest trees, the nation's highest waterfall and the lowest point in the Americas. From snow-capped mountains to sandy deserts, California has it all—even earthquakes. It is one rocking place.

Sounds great! My name is Rick and this is Skipper. We can't wait to see all the things we've heard so much about— giant redwood forests, surfer dudes at the beach and the Hollywood stars!

EARTHQUAKE!

Q. How did California get its name?

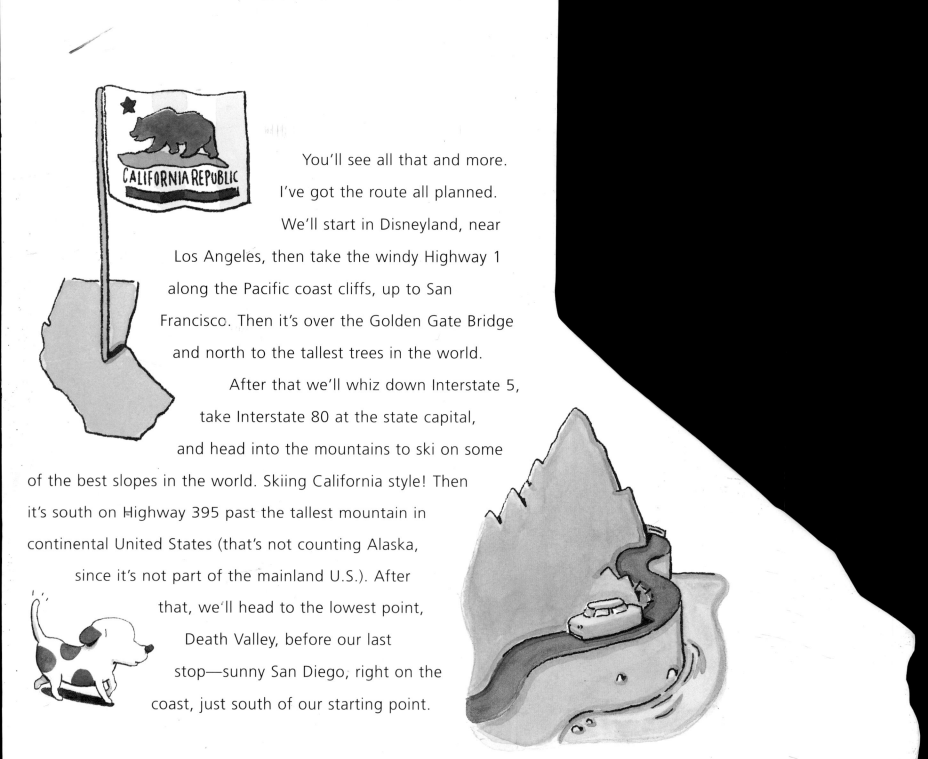

You'll see all that and more. I've got the route all planned. We'll start in Disneyland, near Los Angeles, then take the windy Highway 1 along the Pacific coast cliffs, up to San Francisco. Then it's over the Golden Gate Bridge and north to the tallest trees in the world.

After that we'll whiz down Interstate 5, take Interstate 80 at the state capital, and head into the mountains to ski on some of the best slopes in the world. Skiing California style! Then it's south on Highway 395 past the tallest mountain in continental United States (that's not counting Alaska, since it's not part of the mainland U.S.). After that, we'll head to the lowest point, Death Valley, before our last stop—sunny San Diego, right on the coast, just south of our starting point.

A. From an idyllic island in a 1510 Spanish novel. Spanish explorers gave the name California to the Baja Peninsula in Mexico along the Pacific Coast. The name stuck and was then extended northward to modern California.

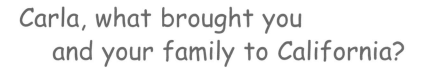

Carla, what brought you and your family to California?

My ancestors moved from Mexico to work in the orange plantations. Today this area is covered with houses and big businesses, but it used to be mainly farms.

That must be why this is called Orange County. Were Mexicans the first people to live in California?

Nope. Native Americans first arrived in California more than 10,000 years ago. People still discover cave drawings by these early inhabitants. In the 1700s, Spanish priests from Mexico were the first Europeans to settle in California. Today, one out of every four people in California is Hispanic and more than four out of ten are minorities.

There are more minorities in California than any other state. It's what helps make California such a dynamic place. A lot of immigrants recently came from places like Mexico, South America and

Q. Why does the California flag have a grizzly bear on it with the words "California Republic"?

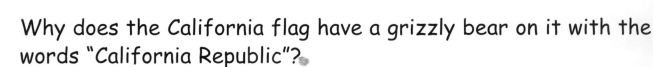

Asia, but many have been here a long, long time. Let's go to the Mission San Juan Capistrano and I'll tell you more about it.

When California was first settled by the Spanish, priests
from Mexico built 21 mis-
sions up and down the
coast. They were a lot like

churches with big ranches. Today, San Juan Capistrano is most famous for its swallows. These birds arrive each year from the South on St. Joseph's Day (March 19th) and depart on St. John's Day (October 23rd).

It's a beautiful place. Did you say this used to be part of Mexico?

Yes, Rick it was. In 1846 the United
States declared war on Mexico. When the
United States Army captured Mexico City,
Mexico surrendered and gave California
and a lot of other land to the United States.

 A. When the settlers from the United States defeated the Mexicans in California in 1846, the settlers' flag had a bear on it, and they proclaimed California the "Bear Flag Republic."

11

Next stop Disneyland! When Walt Disney opened Disneyland in 1955 it was one of the country's first great amusement parks. He filled it with elaborate rides and some of his cartoon characters like Donald Duck, Goofy and Mickey Mouse. Today, it is called the "happiest place on earth."

Well, I'm happy to be here. How did Walt Disney get started?

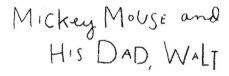

MICKEY MOUSE and HIS DAD, WALT

Walt Disney started making cartoons as a teenager in Illinois. In the 1920s cartoon movies were an exciting new invention, kind of like the Internet today. In 1928, Disney made one of the first talking cartoons. It was called *Steamboat Willie* and it was made for adults—but kids loved it! That's how Mickey Mouse was born, and that was the start of this very happy place. Now let's go to Hollywood to gaze at the stars!

Q. What was Hollywood originally named?

The first Hollywood movie studios came to California in the early 1900s. Film people came because the sunny weather provided good lighting for the films. Plus, they got tans! Pretty soon Hollywood became the most important place for making movies in the world.

I'll say. Hey, there's Mann's Chinese Theater, where actors put their foot or handprints in the cement! There's even a nose print!

That's from the old comedian Jimmy Durante who put his big nose in the wet cement. The most notable person to come out of Hollywood was probably Ronald Reagan, the former president. He started out as an actor (and even made a movie with a monkey!), was later governor of California, and was elected president in 1980.

 "Hollywoodland." The famous sign on the hillside was built in 1923 to advertise a real-estate project, and "-land" fell off after a rainstorm in 1949.

THE CITY of ANGELS

When are we going to see Los Angeles?

You're seeing it! Los Angeles is really a collection of smaller cities. Places like Hollywood, Beverly Hills, Pasadena, Long Beach and Santa Monica are all part of Greater Los Angeles. There are 14 million people altogether, with 3.5 million in the city itself. If Los Angeles County were a country, its economy would be larger than Switzerland's. And it's growing. More immigrants move to Los Angeles every year than any other city in the United States. It's gotten so crowded that a lot of houses have been built on steep hills. When it rains it can really pour, so much so that mudslides wipe out some of those houses.

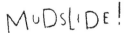

MUDSLIDE!

Q. What strange law was passed in Los Angeles in 1838?

What does Los Angeles mean in Spanish?

"The angels." That's why it's called "The City of Angels." Forty-four settlers from Mexico started Los Angeles in 1781. They called the Mission El Pueblo de Nuestro Señora la Reina de los Angelos del Río Porciúncula (say that three times fast!) after a saint, but pretty much everyone agreed that Los Angeles was a lot easier to say. About 50 years later, more settlers followed, but the trip on foot over the rockies was tough!

After the railroad was built, connecting Los Angeles with the rest of the country by train, the journey to California was much easier. And people really started coming to the city once oil was discovered there in 1892. Since then, the pace of immigration hasn't let up. All these folks means a lot of traffic and smog. For a while, Los Angeles had the worst air pollution in the country.

A. A law banning the unlicensed serenading of women!

15

B ut you can't talk about Los Angeles without talking about beaches, and the center of LA's wacky world of beaches is the Venice Boardwalk in Santa Monica. Venice got its name when a rich man named Abbot Kinney built sixteen miles of canals to drain the area of swamps in the early 1900s. He brought gondolas (skinny boats) from Europe to transport residents and visitors just like the boats in the city of Venice in Italy. Unfortunately, there was an oil spill and most of the canals were paved over. In the 1950s, artists and writers started moving in, leading to the interesting mix of people you see in Venice Beach today.

I've never seen so many palm readers, tarot cards and bikinis in one place! And what's with all the bulging biceps on the weightlifters?

 **Q.** What do chewing gum, baseball and rare plants have in common?

That's Muscle Beach. It used to be called Mussel Beach because of all the mussels (as in shellfish) attached to the piers. But in the 1930s some local workers began an exercise program, and people changed the spelling to reflect the weightlifters' well-oiled torsos.

The famous newspaperman William Randolph Hearst built the most elaborate beach house here, where he threw wild parties in the 1920s and '30s. It had 100 bedrooms, 55 bathrooms and 37 fireplace mantels brought all the way over from England. But enough about Southern California—let's head up north!

 Santa Catalina, an Island off LA's coast. William Wrigley, Jr., famous for his gum, bought the island—home to many exotic plants—in 1919. He used it as the spring-training headquarters for his baseball team, the Chicago Cubs.

Highways. Highways. Highways. There sure are a lot of them! It's not just in Los Angeles, but going all the way up the coast.

There are more than 160,000 miles of paved roads in California— enough to circle the globe six times. In the late 1940s, California started building roads very quickly to accommodate its exploding population and the growing number of cars. All those cars caused a lot of pollution. California now has the world's strictest gasoline standards and leads the movement for electric cars, which are safer for the environment than gas-burning cars.

Plus, some of these highways are beautiful, especially those along the coast, like Highway 1. The Pacific Ocean keeps temperatures along the coast warm in the winter and cool in the summer.

ELECTRIC CARS

Q. How many people live in California?

Sounds like California weather is pretty great. But what about the earthquakes?

There's no getting around that geological wrinkle. Two tectonic plates—basically giant slabs of rock thousands of miles wide underneath the ground—meet along the California coast on something called

TECTONIC PLATES

the San Andreas Fault. When one slips beneath the other, we feel the earth move on top.

Small earthquakes are pretty common. At first they're spooky, but you get used to them. Sometimes there will be a much larger shift, and then it's *really* scary. In 1906, a major earthquake destroyed most of San Francisco. And in 1989, a devastating earthquake struck San Francisco, killing dozens of people and destroying buildings and highways. It also delayed the World Series for ten days.

RUMBLE-TINKLE

More than 33 million people—the most of any state in the Union, and more than the whole country of Canada!

19

Onward we go to Santa Cruz, south of San Francisco, where elephant seals play on the beach. From September to April every year, seals converge at Point Año Nuevo State Reserve.

Carla, they're gigantic—bigger than buffaloes! Why do the really big ones keep bumping into each other?

Those are the males fighting to see who is the toughest. They are big! They can weigh as much as three tons (or about as much as 120 eight-year-old kids)!

In the 1800s, seal hunters almost wiped them out of existence. Only one colony of elephant seals survived in the islands off Mexico's Pacific Coast. With help from animal lovers, the colony continues to grow to this day. They've even become so comfortable some were once found wandering around the second floor of a nearby house!

THUP
THUP

AAARP

Q. How long were the teeth on a saber-toothed tiger?

Are there other interesting animals to see?

You bet, Rick. California has 283 endangered species, more than any other state, and some of the most unusual animals in the world. From the beaches you can sometimes see 50-ton gray whales migrating back and forth from Alaska to Mexico. The giant Pacific octopus off the coast is the world's largest octopus, and it typically weighs between 25 and 35 pounds. Some fishermen once found one that weighed an incredible 600 pounds and had arms that stretched 31 feet.

The California condor, which was also almost driven into extinction, is the largest bird in the world, with wingspans of 9–10 feet. Peregrine falcons, the fastest birds in the world, nest at the Salton Sea National Wildlife Refuge. They can fly as fast as 220 miles per hour in a dive, or four times the speed limit on most highways!

the FALCON WINS!

 Upwards of 8 inches! The tigers lived in California thousands of years ago and their long teeth resembled small swords.

Next up is Silicon Valley—one of the wealthiest areas in the world, thanks to the booming computer industry!

Great! Where's the silicon?
(And what is it, anyway?)

Silicon is a basic element used for silicon chips—important parts inside computers. This area, which stretches from San Jose to Palo Alto, is considered the birthplace of the modern computer.

Silicon Valley first got its start as a technological mecca in 1937 when two Stanford University graduates, William Hewlett and David Packard, began an electronic workshop from a second-story garage in Palo Alto. Their business, Hewlett-Packard, became one of the largest makers of electronic equipment in the world. You can still visit the garage today.

Q. Where in California can you find more than 20,000 Barbie dolls?

Then in the 1970s, Steve Jobs invented the modern computer and started Apple Computer. With those two companies and the hundreds of smaller businesses that followed in their footsteps, Silicon Valley became the center of the technology revolution. Technology is king here. They've even named streets after computer pioneers. The Children's Discovery Museum, which has all sorts of computer games, gadgets and displays for kids, is on Woz Way, named after Steve Wozniak, who founded Apple Computers with Steve Jobs.

Nearby at Stanford University, all kinds of hi-tech experiments take place. In one, scientists use a two-mile tube to bounce atoms traveling at the speed of light off one another, hoping to find quarks, the smallest known particles in the universe.

Sounds tricky!

It is. Only a handful of very smart scientists know exactly how it's done.

 At the Barbie Hall of Fame in Palo Alto. They've got Barbie, Ken and their friends in everything from stretch limousines to exercise gyms.

This must be San Francisco. It sure is a beautiful city.

The steep hills, handsome buildings, morning fog, ocean air and the beautiful San Francisco Bay make for a great postcard. All those things help make it, as people say, "Everyone's favorite city." But it hasn't always been that way.

In the late 1700s, San Francisco was little more than a small religious community. Then, in 1848, boom! Gold was discovered in the mountains east of San Francisco, and everything changed. The city became the hustling, bustling home base for seekers of gold, and it went from 800 people to 25,000 almost overnight.

They weren't all nice people, either. Rough-and-tumble miners, thieves and murderers made San Francisco one of the most sinful cities in the world. One section of San Francisco was called the Barbary Coast after an area in northern Africa that sheltered pirates. The Barbary Coast included places with scary names like Devil's Acre, Deadman's Alley and Murder Point.

Q. What's the official state dance of California?

Weren't they all happy
and rich because of
all that gold?

GOLD!

Not all of them, Rick. Most of

the people who came looking for gold didn't

find any. And it wasn't until the big earthquake in

1906 that the mayhem really stopped. "The Big One,"

as they like to call it, wiped out the more danger-

ous areas, giving the city an

opportunity to start fresh. The city

slowly recovered, and the Bay Bridge and

the Golden Gate bridge were both built in

the 1930s. In the 1950s and 60s, San Francisco

became a center for people with new political

ideas and others who were seeking alter-

native lifestyles. Today, it's a relatively

wealthy place because of all the successful

technology and Internet businesses in nearby

Silicon Valley.

SAN FRANCISCO in the '60's

A. Swing dancing!

What about Chinatown?
I hear that place is pretty special.

Absolutely. Chinatown is one of the most exciting and interesting parts of San Francisco. It's packed with people, colorful signs, back-street allies and exotic shops. The best time to visit is in late January and early February when the Chinese New Year is celebrated.

Why are there so many
Chinese in San Francisco?

Q. What was special about the 442nd and the 100th Infantries in World War II?

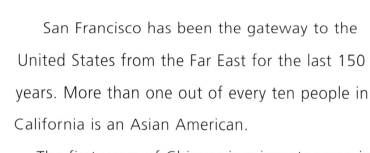

San Francisco has been the gateway to the United States from the Far East for the last 150 years. More than one out of every ten people in California is an Asian American.

The first wave of Chinese immigrants came in the 1860s to help build the first railroad line to cross the entire United States. Tensions arose between the Chinese and the white settlers because many white settlers didn't trust the Chinese, who looked and dressed differently, and had their own language and customs.

That doesn't seem very fair.

It was an ugly period in California history, and it got worse during World War II, when the US was at war with Japan—another country in the Far East. After the Japanese attacked Pearl Harbor in 1941, the government removed 93,000 Japanese Americans from their homes and put them in isolated camps because people were afraid they might help the Japanese. Later, the nation's leaders apologized for this injustice.

A. They were both made up entirely of Japanese Americans. They earned many awards and medals for their hard work and valor.

Time to take in some sites. First up, the Fisherman's Wharf—a virtual paradise for kids. Lots of fishing boats used to use the docks here to bring in their haul of crabs and fish, and some still do today. There's also a whole collection of stores and attractions, including the Ripley's Believe It or Not! Museum and the Guinness Museum of World Records. Silly shops specialize in everything from wind-up toys and sea shells to items for left-handed people only.

Starting in 1990, California sea lions started waddling out of the water and onto Pier 39. Today, you'd think they owned the place. Hundreds of them can usually be seen barking from the pier or basking in the sun.

ARRK

Q. *Clang! Clang! Clang!* goes the trolley. Why do the cable cars ring bells?

What's that island out there?

That's Alcatraz, know to criminals as "The Rock." In the 1930s, the federal government rebuilt what was once an old fortress to hold some of the most dangerous criminals in the land, including legendary gangster Al Capone, Alvin "Creepy" Carpis and Machine Gun Kelly. It was designed to be escape-proof, and many people tried to escape but failed. Today, it's no longer a prison, and you can visit it.

Next stop—Lombard Street.

I've never taken so many turns on one street in my entire life!

And you won't ever again. Lombard Street is known as "the world's crookedest street," taking ten sharp turns before reaching the top of Russian Hill. It used to be as straight as any other street, but it was too steep for cars to drive, so they added the curves in 1922.

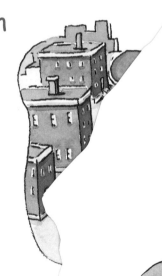

A. Instead of using horns to warn people, the or. bells. There's a cable car bell-ringing champions which driver can ring the bell loudest and in the

Carla, what are all the tracks on the ground for?

Cable cars—another way to make it safe to travel the steep streets. During the mid-19th century, an English mining engineer named Andrew Hallidie watched a horse-drawn carriage slide down one of San Francisco's steep hills. Being an enterprising sort, he built an experimental cable line that guided cars along Clay Street in 1873. It was a big hit. By 1890 there were 500 cable cars covering more than 100 miles of city streets. Today, there are about 40 cable cars on three lines.

Eleven miles of wrapped steel rope—the cable—moves at a steady $9\frac{1}{2}$ miles an hour under the cable car tracks. The cable car driver uses levers to clamp on to the cable through a slot you can see in the road. This moves the cable car forward.

Q. How many painters does it take to keep the Golden Gate Bridge gleaming?

Sounds like the hills sure made
it tough to build a city here.

Yep, but as is usually the case, they found a way!
And now, at last, the Golden Gate Bridge,
San Francisco's best-known feature. It took four years
to build the nearly two-mile-long bridge linking San
Francisco with Marin County to the north. When it
was completed in 1937, it was the longest suspension
bridge in the world. The two towers rising 746 feet
above the water are as tall as a 70-story building. When we walk
across, don't worry if you feel it swinging—it's designed
to sway as much as 27 feet because of the winds
and earthquakes.

It sure is big. Look, Skipper!
You can *barely* see a
painter up top!

A. Twenty-five. Every week they apply 1,000 gallons of paint
to the bridge.

Time to head up to the Point Reyes National Seashore, one of California's most beautiful natural displays. Some people call it an "Island in Time" because, from a naturalist's perspective, time has stopped here. It is a big isolated chunk of land that is gradually moving away from the mainland as the tectonic plates shift.

Two things not to miss. One is Earthquake Trail. You can see a 16-foot gap between what was once a continuous fence until a huge crack emerged during the earthquake of 1906, splitting the fence in two. Now that's power! The other spot is Point Reyes Lighthouse. When the weather is clear, it is the best place on the West Coast to see whales. Of course, you can't always count on the sun shining. Point Reyes gets an average of 2,700 hours of fog every year, or almost eight hours per day.

WHERE ARE the PEOPLE?

Q. Who invented the mountain bike?

Let's see, I've seen a Sir Francis Drake Boulevard, Drake's Bay, Drake's Beach, Drake's Estero and a dozen other Drake-some-things. Who was Drake?

Sir Francis Drake was a British sea captain who landed his ship in California 1579. Before leaving, he claimed the area for England and named it Nova Albion, which means New England in Latin.

The seashore is great, but what can we find inland?

About 20 miles in, you'll find wine country. A Hungarian count named Ágoston Haraszthy launched California into the wine business in 1857. Today, there are about 50 wineries in Sonoma Valley and 230 in Napa Valley. In the 1970s, California wines started beating French wines in international wine-tasting contests!

 A handful of avid bicyclists in northern California invented the mountain bike in the 1970s so they could more easily complete a treacherous 1.8-mile race on Mount Tam in Marin County.

What about the redwood forests? Aren't they somewhere around here?

The redwood forests are home to some spectacular trees—the tallest in the whole world! Probably the best place to see one is the "Avenue of the Giants" at Humboldt Redwoods State Park. There is a 32-mile scenic drive through a forest with some of the biggest redwoods in the world. One of the tallest, coming in at 362 feet high, called the Dyerville Giant, fell in 1991. This tree had a trunk as a thick as a two-story house, and was as tall as a 35-story building!

It takes 500 years for a redwood to reach its full height. The oldest known one is 2,200 years old, dating back to before Jesus was born. The bark is thick and the roots are very shallow; they only go about 6 feet deep, but spread out 80 to 100 feet—kind of like a big upside down nail sitting on its flat head.

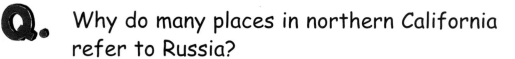

Q. Why do many places in northern California refer to Russia?

34

I bet you could make great
tree houses in them.

Well, Rick, a woman named Julia "Butterfly" Hill lived in a redwood tree for two years, from 1997 until 1999, to protect it from loggers who wanted to cut it down. She named her tree Luna and said "I gave my word to this tree, the forest and to all the people that my feet would not touch the ground until I had done everything in my power to make the world aware of this problem and to stop the destruction." Eventually the tree was saved. Many people admire her for her courage, while others think she's a little nutty.

Julia Butterfly
Lived in a Tree
For Two Years!

I've seen oceans and forests, but are there volcanoes in California?

Yes. Lassen Peak in northeastern California is the world's largest plug-dome volcano. The last eruption was in 1915 when it blew ashes 7 miles into the air! Now let's head over to the Gold Country.

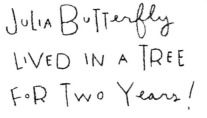

A·Roop
Nyet.

 A. In the early 1800s, the Russian empire extended all the way to northern California. Russian trappers made a living selling the hides of sea otters and seals.

The Gold Country is about 100 miles inland of San Francisco. It's where the great California Gold Rush of 1849 took place, which started when a man named John Marshall was working on a sawmill for John Sutter in 1848. He noticed a shiny rock in the stream. After consulting an encyclopedia, Marshall and Sutter realized it was a gold nugget, about half the size of a pea. News of the discovery spread fast. People from all over the world headed to California hoping to strike it rich. They were called "forty-niners" because many arrived in the spring of 1849.

But how did they find the gold?

There are two types of gold deposits. Lode is gold quartz buried deep beneath the ground. To get to that you dig mines. Placer is a small piece of gold that has moved to the surface of the ground, often in creeks and rivers. Marshall's gold was placer. Because gold is heavier than dirt and sand, it settles to the bottom of pans, which

Q. Who was Charlie Parkhurst?

36

prospectors plunged into the stream beds and swirled around. This is the simplest way to find gold, but there are much more elaborate ways. Armed with heavy picks and pans, prospectors found millions of dollars worth of gold over the next decade. In 1859, a 54-pound nugget was found.

Some people built fortunes without discovering gold. In 1853, Levi Strauss formed a clothing company for miners. By 1874 he had developed a line of heavy work pants that the miners called "Levis." Today we call those blue jeans!

Wow! Sounds like the discovery of gold sure was a great event for California.

Well, Rick, not everybody benefited. Many prospectors left empty handed. Both Marshall and Sutter died penniless because other miners sneaked onto their land and took all the gold.

And now, on to Sacramento—the capital of California.

A. A great stagecoach driver in the late-19th century, and a tough character with whom few cared to start trouble. Upon Charlie's death in 1879, it was discovered that *he* was a woman.

Carla, if Los Angeles and San Francisco are bigger, how come Sacramento is the capitol?

Because it's near the Gold Country, Rick, and back when they were selecting the city that would be California's capital, that was a pretty important thing. Although there are some places where you can still pan for riches in the Gold Country, today most of the gold is gone. Instead, Sacramento is a thriving city that is the center of the state government. It's also part of California's Great Central Valley, one of the most important farming regions in the world.

SACRAMENTO

I didn't know California was an important farm state.

It sure is. There are thousands and thousands of farms in the Great Central Valley, a vast 430-mile flat region that borders the Sierra Nevada Mountains to

Q. Why is "Eureka" the state motto?

the east and the Coastal Mountain Range to the west. There are two main sections: the Sacramento Valley in the north and the San Joaquin Valley in the south.

What crops do Califonia farmers grow?

All kinds of stuff. The region grows the most broccoli (blech!), carrots, cauliflower (double blech!), celery, lettuce, lima beans and spinach in the United States, and the vast majority of the nation's almonds, dates, figs, nectarines, olives and walnuts. Other major crops include cotton, roses, peaches, avocados, melons, plums, strawberries and tomatoes. In all, farmers grow more than 200 crops here.

Fresno County alone in the San Joaquin Valley has about 8,000 farms, more than any other county in the nation, and is the leading producer of tomatoes, grapes, and cotton.

EUREKA!

A. Eureka means "I have found it" in Greek. When prospectors found gold in the 1850s, they often shouted "Eureka!" The word is also on the state seal and is the name of a city in northern California.

And farming isn't limited to the Great Valley. Monterey County on the coast is the leading grower of lettuce and is known as the "Salad Bowl of the World." In southern California, Riverside County produces the most eggs, San Bernardino County has the most milk cows, and Imperial County grows the most hay.

Wow. I never thought
of farmers when I thought
of California before.
Who are all those people
in the fields?

Q. Where can you experience an earthquake, but without the danger?

Those are migrant workers, who move from farm to farm harvesting crops. One of California's most important men came from these fields. Cesar Chavez picked fruits and vegetables as a child.

Angry about the poor pay and terrible working conditions, Chavez started the United Farms Workers of America when he grew up. Chavez used hunger strikes, protest marches and boycotts to make people pay attention to the problems of migrant workers. His efforts helped raise wages, bring water and toilets into fields, control the use of pesticides and inspire the civil rights movement for Mexican Americans and other people from Latin America. And he's not just my hero, either—San Francisco recently named one of its major streets after him!

CESAR CHAVEZ

I guess it's not just crops that California's Great Central Valley has produced—some amazing people, too!

 An earthquake simulator at the California Science Center in Los Angeles let's out-of-town visitors experience an earthquake without actually having to live through the real thing.

41

Next stop is the Sierra Nevadas, a 400-mile long granite block of spectacular mountains that will make your jaw drop from the sheer majesty of it. It is an outdoor enthusiast's paradise with glacial lakes, plunging cliffs, roaring waterfalls and endless hiking trails.

In the north, we have Lake Tahoe, which crosses the Nevada border. On Nevada's side there are casinos where gambling is legal. California's side of the lake boasts fourteen ski resorts. Most people think surfing when they ponder California's recreational activities, but California also offers some of the best skiing in the country.

There is also some spooky history. One group of settlers, called the Donner Party, set out on a journey to California in 1846. They took a suggested "short cut," and ended up getting stuck near a lake (now called Donner Lake) when the worst winter in a century struck, dumping 20 feet of snow and stranding them in the mountains. When they were finally rescued the following spring, only 40 out of the original 87 had survived.

Q. How does Native American legend say that Half Dome and Full Dome (another rock formation in Yosemite) were formed?

That sounds like a party I wouldn't want to go to. Don't you have anything more pleasant to tell me about?

Sure, Yosemite National Park!

Awesome!

You bet. Waterfalls cascade 3,000 feet from those cliffs. Granite mountain peaks loom over pristine lakes and flower-covered meadows. Sweeping views reveal green forests with massive 300-foot-tall sequoia trees. On one side of Yosemite Valley you see Half Dome, a massive cliff. On the other side is the imposing El Captain, one giant slab of granite. The two highest waterfalls in the nation, Yosemite Falls and Ribbon Falls, are both here.

YOSEMITE NATIONAL PARK

A. According to the legend, the great spirits turned a quarreling wife and husband into the mammoth Half Dome and Full Dome rock formations. Tears from the wife (Half Dome) formed Mirror Lake below.

43

MT. WHITNEY

Farther south is Mount Whitney—at 14,494 feet above sea level, the highest mountain peak in the continental United States. About 2,000 people climb it each year. What's really amazing is that Death Valley, the lowest point in North and South America, is in the very same county, Inyo County.

Wow! California has some strange geography!

DEATH VALLEY

It doesn't take long to find a complete contrast, if that's what you mean. We could drive to Badwater at the bottom of Death Valley, 282 feet below sea level, fry an egg on the hood of the car and then drive back into the mountains to quick-freeze it in a snow bank. The hottest temperature ever recorded in North America was at Death Valley. It once hit 134°F. And it almost never rains—less than 2 inches each year.

Q. **Where can you find the oldest living thing on Earth?**

I think I can guess why it's called Death Valley.

Well, you wouldn't want to get stuck there if your car ran out of gas. If the sun doesn't get you during the day, the cool weather makes it awfully chilly during the night. When people go to the desert, they better be prepared and better bring extra water. A fourth of California is covered by desert, and though you might not think it, some of the deserts are very beautiful, and attract visitors year round.

And ways have been developed to bring water to the deserts through irrigation. In some cases, giant sprinklers can spread water across huge streches of land so that crops can be grown there.

A. In California's Inyo National Forest. There, some of the Great Basin bristlecone pine trees are more than 4,000 years old.

That brings us to our last stop, San Diego.

Back to where we started, right?

Right. This completes the circle: Not only are we back where we started, but San Diego is both California's oldest community and newest big city. In 1542, San Diego Bay was the first place Spanish

ships entered California, and it was where the first mission was established in 1769. One reason it took so long for the Spanish to settle California from Mexico is because the ocean current and winds made it difficult for ships to sail north along the West Coast.

Once settled, San Diego took a long time to flourish. The gold rush, oil boom and film industry all bypassed the city. But when the Japanese bombed Pearl Harbor

Q. What did the famous stagecoach robber Black Bart leave at the scene of his heists?

in 1941, the Navy moved the headquarters of its Pacific Fleet to San Diego. Between that and its rapidly growing aviation industry, San Diego took off.

Check out all the surfing dudes on the beach!

When people talk about the laid-back California lifestyle, they're talking about San Diego more than any other place. More sunny days than any other place else in the country, temperatures that almost never get too hot or too cold, sandy beaches right in the center of the city and a easygoing outlook on life make San Diego a relaxed and wonderful place to live. Plus, there are tons of things to do between the San Diego Zoo (one of the best in the world), the deserts inland, the exotic sights nearby in Tijuana, Mexico, and, of course, the ocean.

I know it isnt funny, But I Just took all your money
Black Bart PO8

A. Poems. He got his name from the bits of poetry he left behind at each crime, signed: "Black Bart, PO8" (Poet).

Well, that's it. California in a nut shell. I wish we had more time. We missed loads of interesting places and nuggets of history, but I think we covered the main parts.

We've seen so much. It's hard to believe there could be more!

Believe it or not, Rick, there is. From mountain men to movie stars, California has seen it all. It's a place where almost anything is possible, both in the incredible contrasts of the natural world, as well as the people who live here.

MOUNTAIN MEN

MOVIE STARS

Yep, California sure has every-thing, and it seems like every day brings something new.

Q. How many members of the famous rock 'n' roll group "The Beach Boys" could actually surf?

One hundred and fifty years ago, California was just a collection of dusty missions. Today, it's the eighth largest economy in the world, and one of the most diverse collections of people. And they just keep coming! By boat, by plane, by car or by train, it's the ultimate land of opportunity.

Thanks a million, Carla. It's been a blast! Skipper and I can't wait to come back and learn more!

 A. Only one! But that didn't stop them from recording some smash hits like "Surfin' Safari" and "Surfin' U.S.A."

STATE SHAPES